DO YOU REALLY WANT TO VISIT JUPITER?

BY BRIDGET HEOS

ILLUSTRATED BY DANIELE FABBRI

amicus
illustrated

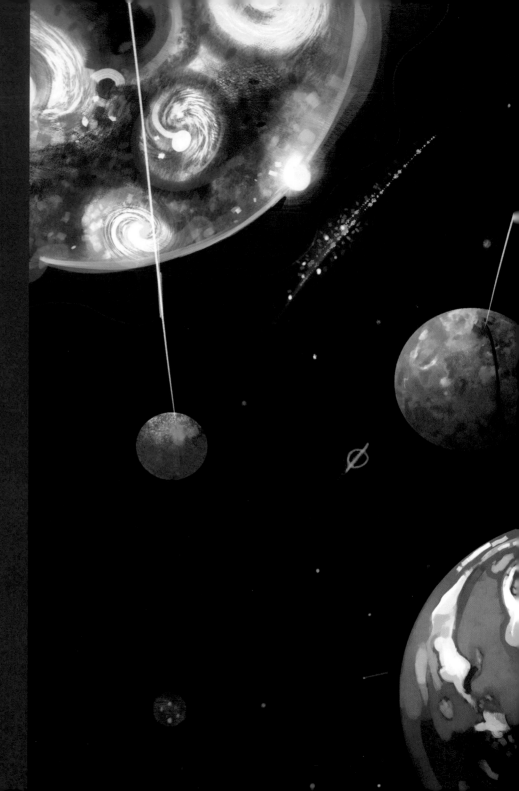

Amicus Illustrated is published by Amicus
P.O. Box 1329, Mankato, MN 56002
www.amicuspublishing.us

Library of Congress Cataloging-in-Publication Data
Heos, Bridget.
Do you really want to visit Jupiter? / by Bridget Heos;
illustrated by Daniele Fabbri. — 1st ed.
  p. cm. — (Do you really want to visit—?)
Audience: K-3.
Summary: "A child astronaut takes an imaginary trip to
Jupiter, learns about the harsh conditions on the biggest
planet, and decides that Earth is a good home after
all. Includes solar system diagram, Jupiter vs. Earth fact
chart, and glossary"–Provided by publisher.
 Includes bibliographical references.
ISBN 978-1-60753-199-9 (library binding) —
ISBN 978-1-60753-405-1 (ebook)
1. Jupiter (Planet)—Juvenile literature. 2. Jupiter
(Planet)—Exploration—Juvenile literature. I. Fabbri,
Daniele, 1978– ill. II. Title. III. Series: Do you really
want to visit—?
QB661.H46 2014
523.45–dc23   2012025971

Editor: Rebecca Glaser
Designer: The Design Lab

Printed in the United States of America at
Corporate Graphics in North Mankato, Minnesota.

Date 4/2014   PO 1219

9 8 7 6 5 4 3

3

So you say you want to go to Jupiter. You'd really like to live there. But do you *really* want to go to Jupiter?

Jupiter is hundreds of millions of miles away, and it will take you five or six years to get there. Better pack snacks! And the world's best space suit. Jupiter is a dangerous place.

When you reach the planet, bundle up! At its outer edge, Jupiter is twice as cold as anywhere on Earth.

5

Hold onto your hat! The stripes are clouds whipping around the planet—faster than an F5 tornado. Luckily, your spaceship can withstand heavy winds. Just don't open the...

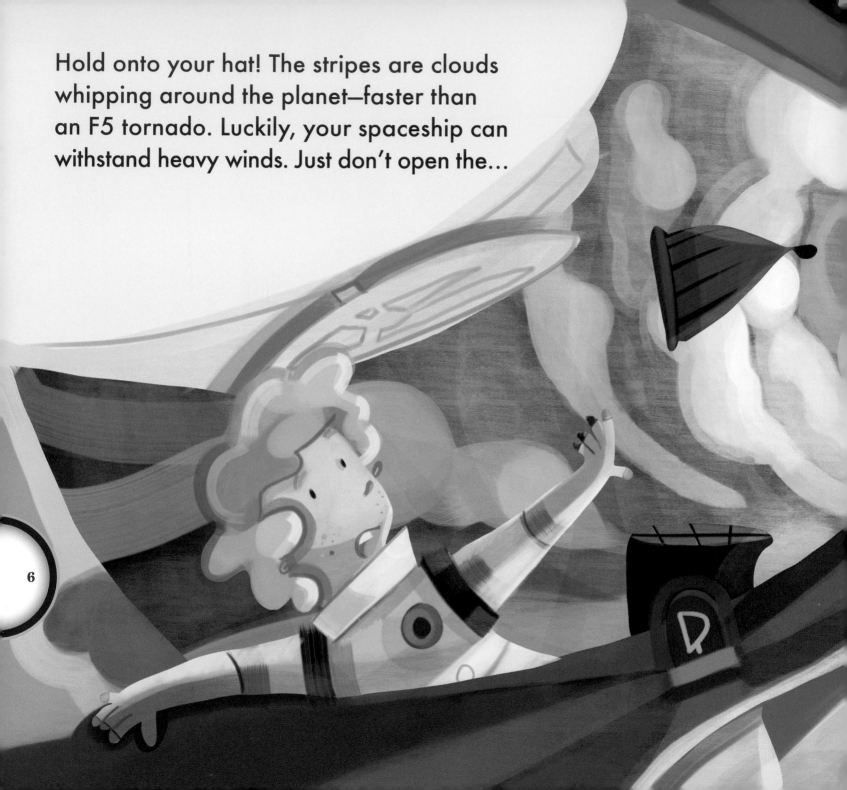

Whatever you do, stay away from the Great Red Spot. It's a hurricane as big as two Earths. It's been raging for hundreds of years.

Unfortunately, there is nothing solid to grasp to avoid blowing away. Jupiter is made up of gas 12,400 miles (20,000 km) deep. It's one of the "gas giants," along with Saturn, Uranus, and Neptune (and the fifth grader who ate baked beans for lunch).

You'll need an oxygen tank. On Jupiter, the air is mostly hydrogen and helium. On the plus side, these gases are great for balloons.

As you travel through the gas, temperature rises and pressure builds. Make sure your space suit can protect you from being crushed! The balloons won't be so lucky.

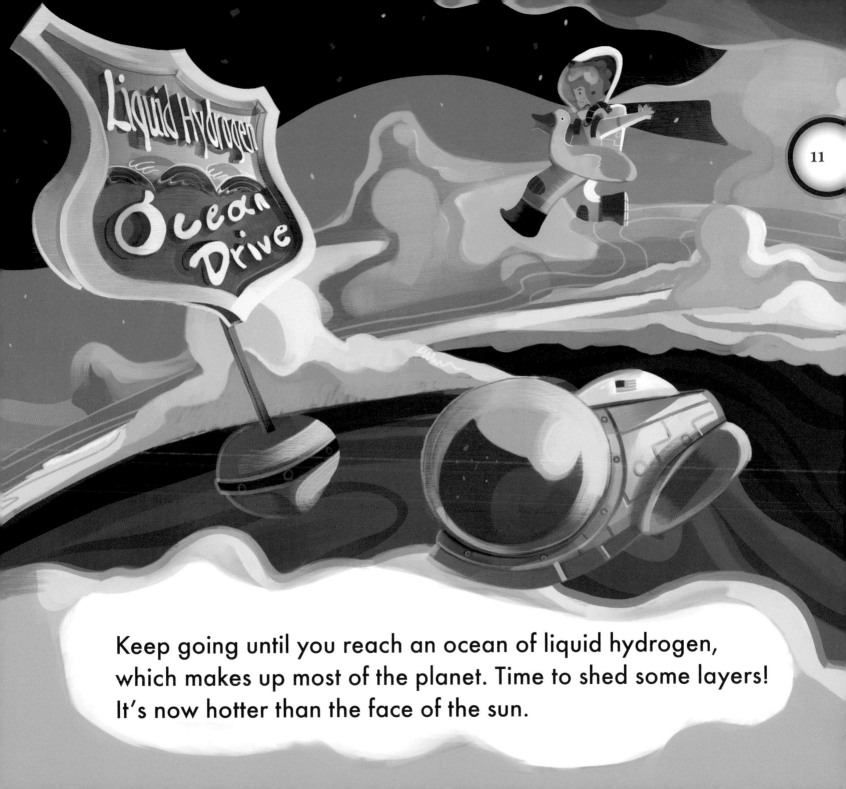

Keep going until you reach an ocean of liquid hydrogen, which makes up most of the planet. Time to shed some layers! It's now hotter than the face of the sun.

Aah. The ocean can be so relaxing. Just don't try to cool off in the molten metal! And don't bother looking for seashells. The whole planet is a metallic ocean— with no beach! No life could survive here.

Wait a second. What are you doing here? Quick, back in the spaceship! Maybe touring Jupiter's many moons would be safer. As you fly away, note how Jupiter fills your whole view. By far the biggest planet, it could hold 1,400 Earths!

Zoom past football-shaped Metis and other inner moons to reach the Galilean moons—the big kahunas. Io looks like a giant pizza. Mmm.

14

Watch out! That's hot lava shooting out of Io's more than 80 volcanoes. It can travel 180 miles (290 km) into space!

Whew! That was a close one. Europa is a nice change of pace. Its surface is made of ice. Below lies an ocean. Out of snacks? Try ice fishing. You'll need a long drill—the ice may be a few miles thick! But who knows what tasty creature you'll hook!

Travel farther to Jupiter's many tiny moons.
You could walk around one in about an hour.

What's the matter?
Oh, I see. Earth is your home.

There. That's better.
Home sweet pizza parlor.

19

Jupiter was breathtaking,
but you really wouldn't
want to live there.

20

URANUS

NEPTUNE

SATURN

MARS

EARTH

JUPITER

VENUS

MERCURY

SUN

21

How Do We Know About Jupiter?

We can't actually go to Jupiter. A spaceship that could travel almost 400 million miles (644 million km) and back doesn't exist yet. Instead, space probes have been sent to take photos and measurements. They include *Pioneer 10* (1973) and *Pioneer 11* (1974), *Voyagers 1* and *2* (1979), and *Galileo* (1995–2003). The newest spacecraft, *Juno*, will arrive at Jupiter in 2016.

Earth vs. Jupiter

	Earth	Jupiter
Position in solar system	Third from Sun	Fifth from Sun
Average distance from Sun	93 million miles (150 million km)	483 million miles (778 million km)
Year (time to orbit Sun)	365 days	11.86 Earth years
Day (sunrise to sunrise)	24 hours	9.925 Earth hours
Diameter	7,926 miles (12, 756 km)	88,846 miles (142,984 km)
Mass	1	317.83 times Earth
Air	Oxygen and nitrogen	Hydrogen and helium
Water	About 70% covered with water	Likely has water vapor in clouds, which might sustain life—but not humans
Moons	1	63 known moons
Pizza	Earth has pizza.	Io looks like pizza, but is not pizza!

Glossary

F5 tornado The most damaging level of tornado measured on the Fujita scale, with winds of 216–318 mph (419–512 km/h).

Galilean moons Jupiter's four largest moons, discovered in 1610 by scientist Galileo. They are Io, Ganymede, Europa, and Callisto.

gas The form of a substance in which it expands to fill a given area.

helium A light colorless gas that does not burn. It is often used to fill balloons.

hydrogen A colorless gas that is lighter than air and catches fire easily. It can also be used to fill balloons, but it's not recommended.

lava The hot, liquid rock of a volcano.

liquid The form of a substance in which it flows freely, but unlike a gas, does not expand freely.

moon A body that circles around a planet.

oxygen A colorless gas that humans and animals need to breathe and is essential to life.

planet A large body that revolves around a sun.

pressure The weight of air or water pressing down on something.

temperature How hot or cold something is.

volcano A vent on the surface of a planet or moon through which lava from underground flows.

Read More

Aguilar, David A. *11 Planets: A New View of the Solar System*. National Geographic, 2008.

Grego, Peter. *Voyage through Space*. Space Guides. QEB Publishing, 2007.

Hansen, Rosanna. *Jupiter*. Early Bird Astronomy. Lerner, 2010.

Mist, Rosalind. *Jupiter and Saturn*. Solar System. QEB Publishing, 2009.

Owens, L.L. *Jupiter*. Child's World, 2011.

Websites

Mission to Jupiter: NASA's The Space Place
http://spaceplace.nasa.gov/junoquest/en/
Learn about *Juno*, the next space probe that will visit Jupiter, and what scientists hope to learn from it.

NASA Kids' Club
http://www.nasa.gov/audience/forkids/kidsclub/flash/
NASA Kids' Club features games, pictures, and information about astronauts and space travel.

StarChild: A Learning Center for Young Astronomers
http://starchild.gsfc.nasa.gov/docs/StarChild/
Click on Solar System to read facts about all the planets.

Welcome to the Planets: Jupiter
http://pds.jpl.nasa.gov/planets/choices/jupiter1.htm
View slideshows of the best photographs taken of Jupiter, plus hear captions read aloud.

24

About the Author

Bridget Heos is the author of more than 40 books for children and teens, including *What to Expect When You're Expecting Larvae* (2011, Lerner). She lives in Kansas City with husband Justn, sons Johnny, Richie, and J.J., plus a dog, cat, and Guinea pig. You can visit her online at www.authorbridgetheos.com.

About the Illustrator

Daniele Fabbri was born in Ravenna, Italy, in 1978. He graduated from Istituto Europeo di Design in Milan, Italy, and started his career as cartoon animator, storyboarder, and background designer for animated series. He has worked as a freelance illustrator since 2003, collaborating with international publishers and advertising agencies.